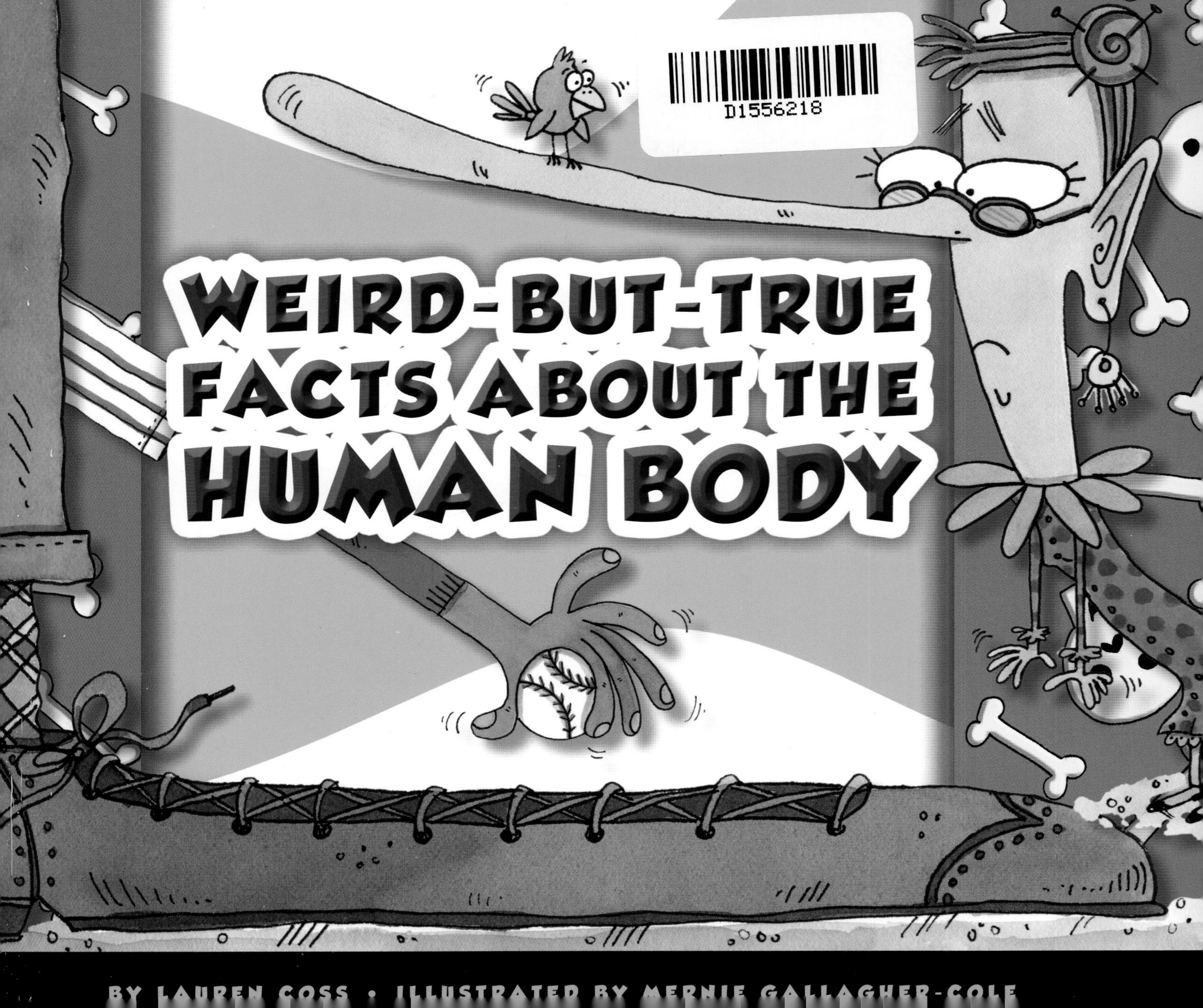

BY LAUREN COSS • ILLUSTRATED BY MERNIE GALLAGHER-COLE

Published by RiverStream Publishing
PO Box 364
Mankato, MN 56002
www.riverstreampublishing.com

RiverStream Publishing reprinted with permission of The Child's World®.

ISBN 9781614734192
LCCN 2012946526

Printed in the United States of America
Mankato, MN

1 2 3 4 5 CG 16 15 14 13
RiverStream Publishing—Corporate Graphics,
Mankato, MN—022014—1051CGW14

About the Author

Lauren Coss is an author and editor living in Saint Paul, Minnesota. She has some of her best ideas while dreaming.

About the Illustrator

A former greeting card artist, Mernie Gallagher-Cole is a freelance illustrator with over 28 years experience illustrating for children. Her charming illustrations can be found on greeting cards, party goods, games, puzzles, children's books, and now e-books and educational game apps! She lives in Philadelphia with her husband and two children.

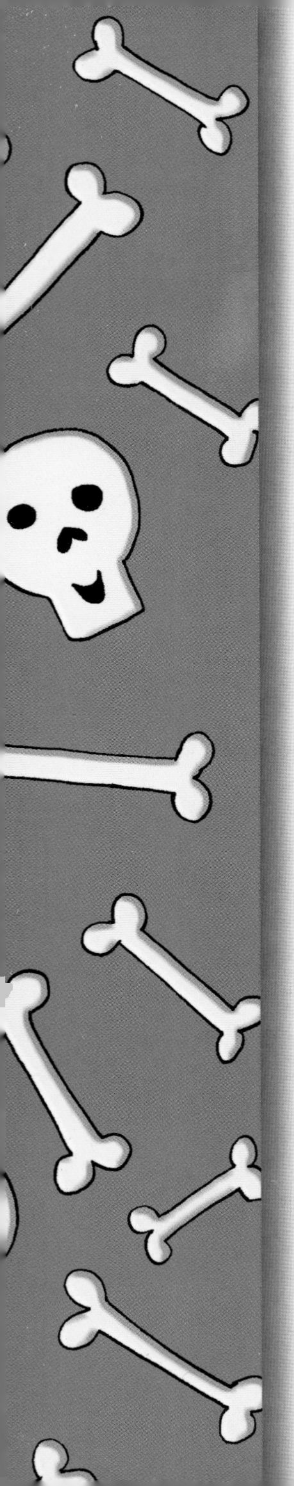

TABLE OF CONTENTS

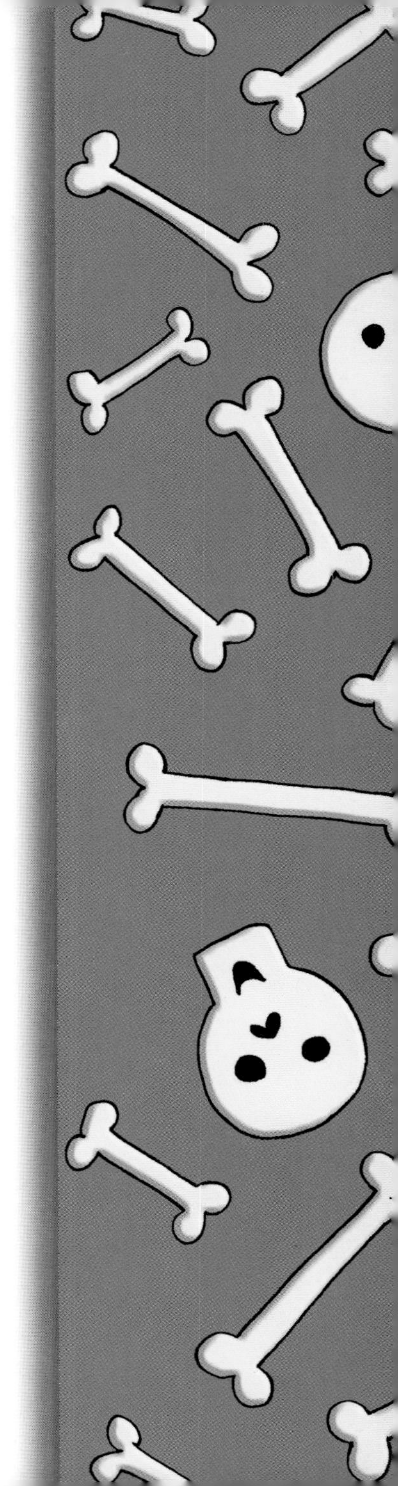

INTRODUCTION

From head to toe, there is more going on inside and outside of you than meets the eye. The human body can be a weird and wild place. From tongue prints to fuzzy intestines, the human body involves all kinds of weird-but-true facts. Get ready to learn all about the incredible human body. And remember, even though these facts might seem too bizarre to believe, they are all true!

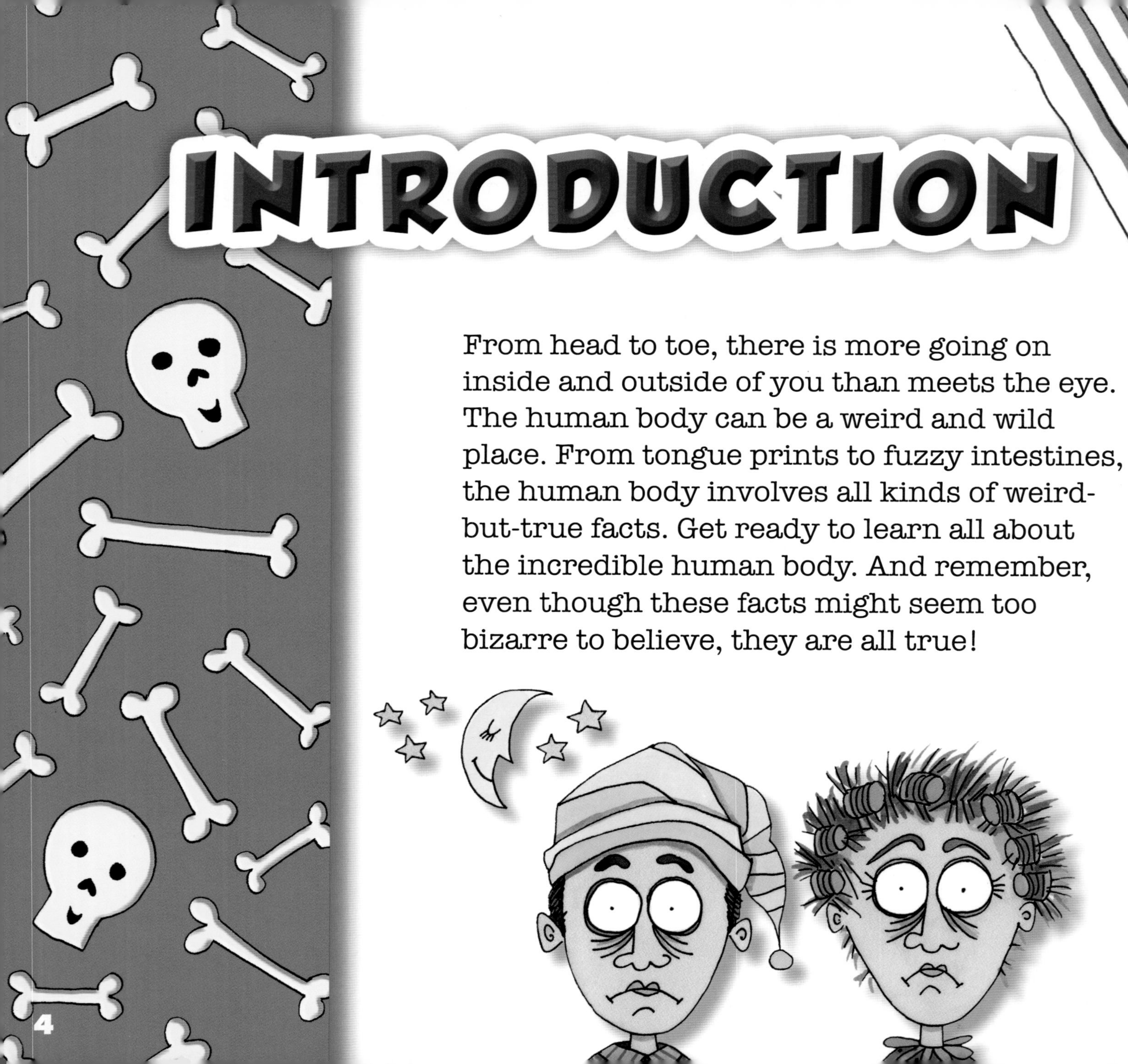

HEAD ESSENTIALS

The human brain is bright pink.

The average human brain weighs only 3 pounds (1.4 kg).

That's less than half the weight of an average human's skin.

Many great thinkers have claimed to get some of their best ideas while snoozing.

Dmitri Mendeleev, who created the periodic table of elements, said the idea for the organization of the table came to him in a dream. Studies have shown dreaming is linked to memory and learning. Researchers speculate that dreams help people make sense of what they saw or did during the day.

Listening to Mozart doesn't actually make you smarter.

A 1990s study suggested that students who listened to music by Wolfgang Amadeus Mozart scored higher on IQ tests. However, the results from the study have never been reproduced. There is no scientific proof the music has any effect on intelligence.

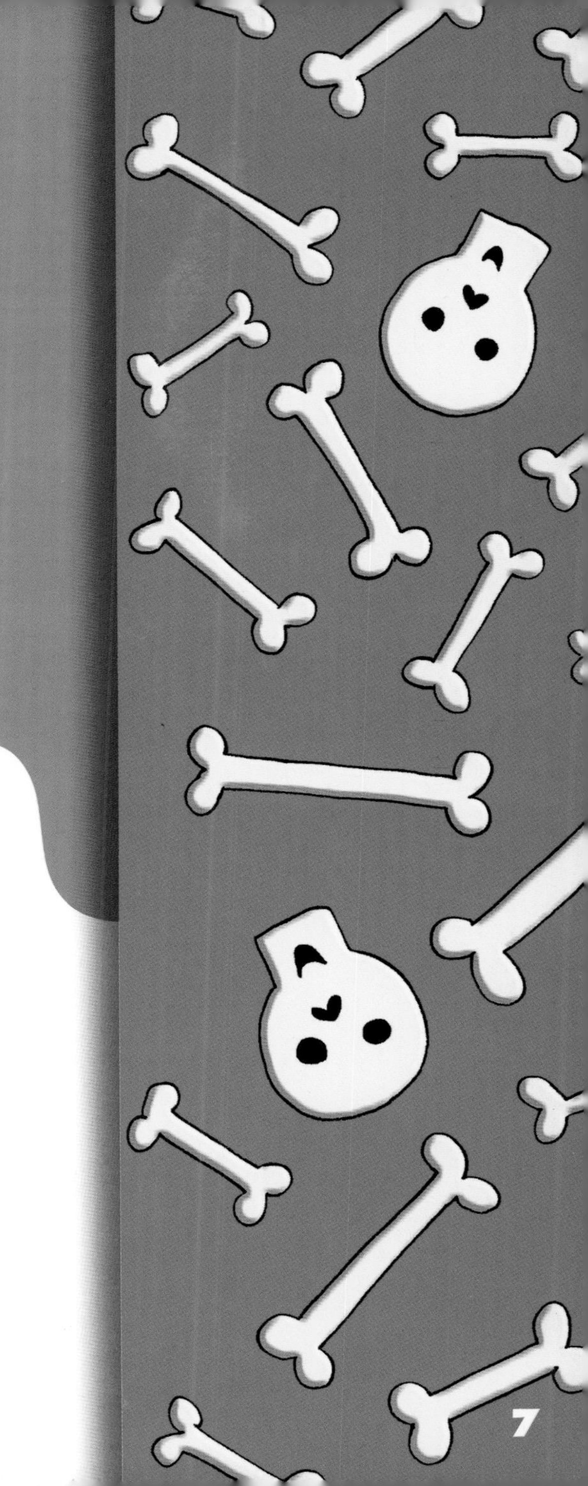

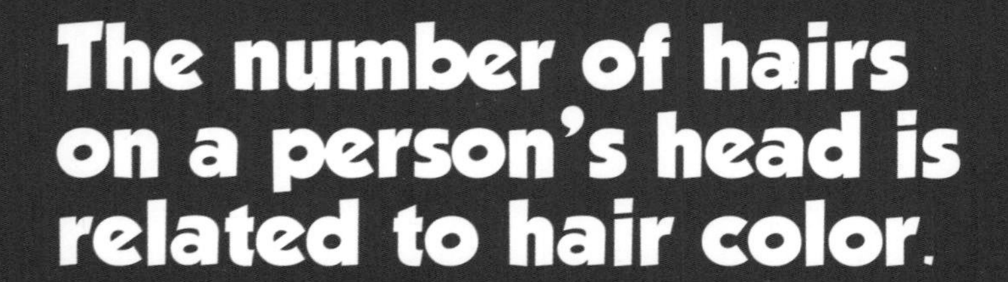

The number of hairs on a person's head is related to hair color.

On average, blonds have the most hair **follicles**. Redheads have the least.

Curly hair tangles less than straight hair.

Straight hair tends to be finer than curly hair, which makes it more likely to knot up.

Human hair is extremely strong.

Each strand of hair can support 3.5 ounces (100 g). Together, the hair from an average head could support the weight of at least two elephants.

Most people lose an average of 100 hairs every day.

It's no wonder your shower drain gets clogged sometimes!

In 2007, a man pulled an airplane using only his ears.

Great Britain's Manjit Singh pulled the 41-passenger plane 12 feet (3.9 m). He used a harness attached to his ears to lug the 7.4-ton (6.8 t) aircraft.

People have been piercing their ears for thousands of years.

In 1991, the remains of a man who had lived more than 5,000 years ago were discovered in an Italian glacier. The man, nicknamed Ötzi, had both his earlobes pierced.

The part of the world your family came from determines what type of earwax you have.

There are two kinds of earwax: sticky and dry. People of European or African descent usually have sticky earwax. People of Asian or American Indian ancestry usually have dry earwax. Scientists can study earwax to help them figure out how early humans traveled around the world.

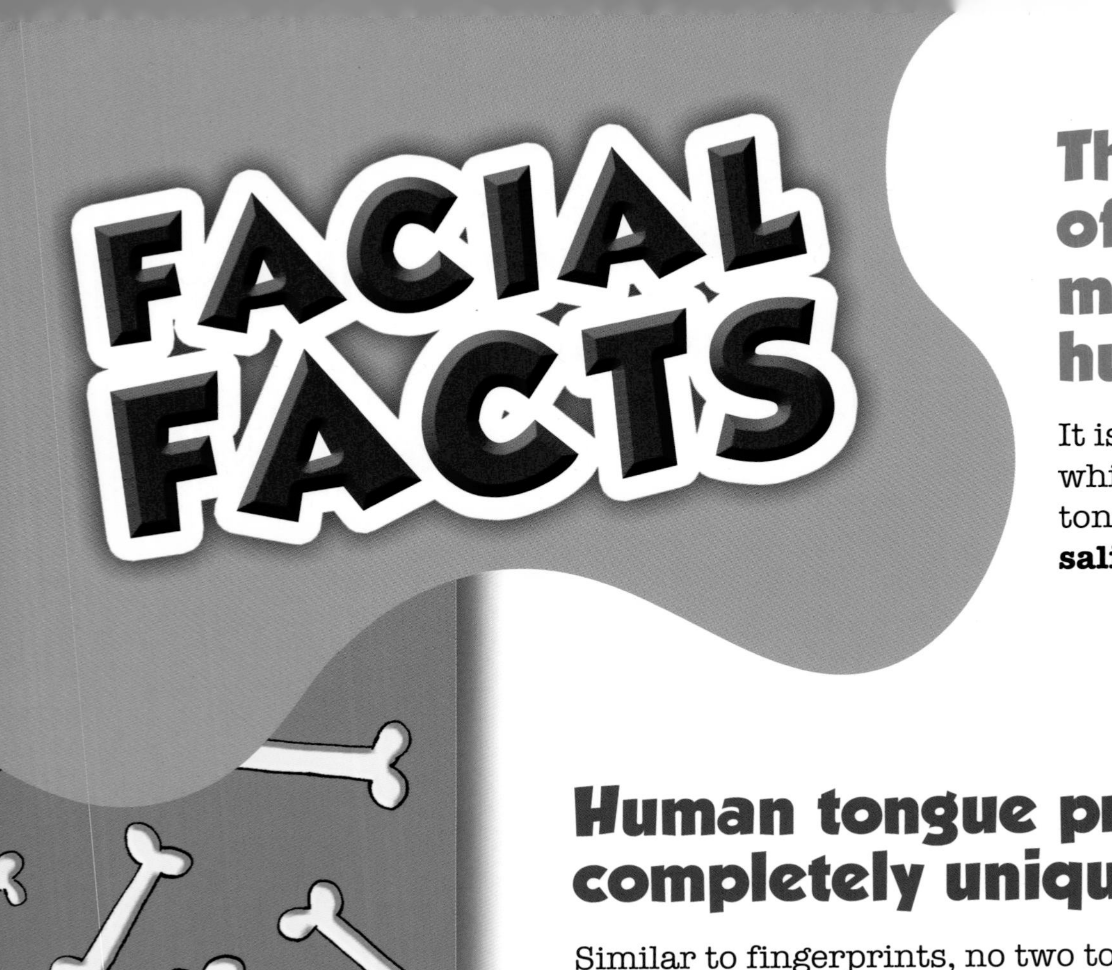

The tongue is one of the strongest muscles in the human body.

It is also one of the busiest. Even while you are sleeping, your tongue is hard at work pushing **saliva** down your throat.

Human tongue prints are completely unique.

Similar to fingerprints, no two tongue prints are alike.

Dimples form in unborn babies when a tiny area of skin attaches to the muscle below.

Your nose and ears will keep getting bigger for the rest of your life.

Most people's bones are fully formed by the time they are 25 years old. But your ears and most of your nose are made of **cartilage**, which never stops growing.

An average human makes enough spit in a lifetime to fill two swimming pools.

This is equal to about 25,000 quarts (24,000 L) of saliva.

A human nose can detect more than 10,000 smells.

This may sound like a lot, but it's nothing compared to other animals. Some dogs have a sense of smell more than 100,000 times better than a human's.

One in three humans sneeze when they look at the sun or another bright light.

This is called photic sneezing.

You can't outrun a sneeze.

The tiny liquid particles in an average sneeze travel more than 35 miles per hour (56 km/h).

On average, women have a stronger sense of smell than men.

You can't sneeze while you are asleep.

Humans sneeze when a dust, pollen, or other particle irritates the inside of their noses. When you are sleeping, the nerves that detect these irritants are also resting.

The muscles around the eyes are the most active in the human body.

These muscles never take a break. They even move when you are asleep. Researchers estimate your eyes move 100,000 times a day!

An average human eyelash has a lifespan of five months.

After that, the eyelash falls out. An average human has 200 lashes on each eye. The lashes help protect the eye from dust and other debris.

Adults blink much more often than babies.

Babies blink about once a minute. The average adult, however, blinks at least 15 times a minute. Blinking helps clear your eyes of dust and debris and keeps them damp.

Your eyes see everything upside down.

Light comes in and is flipped upside down by the lenses in your eyes. But when the information about the image you saw gets to your brain, your brain turns the image the right direction.

INSIDE AND OUT

If stretched out, an adult human's small intestines can reach 25 feet (7.6 m) long.

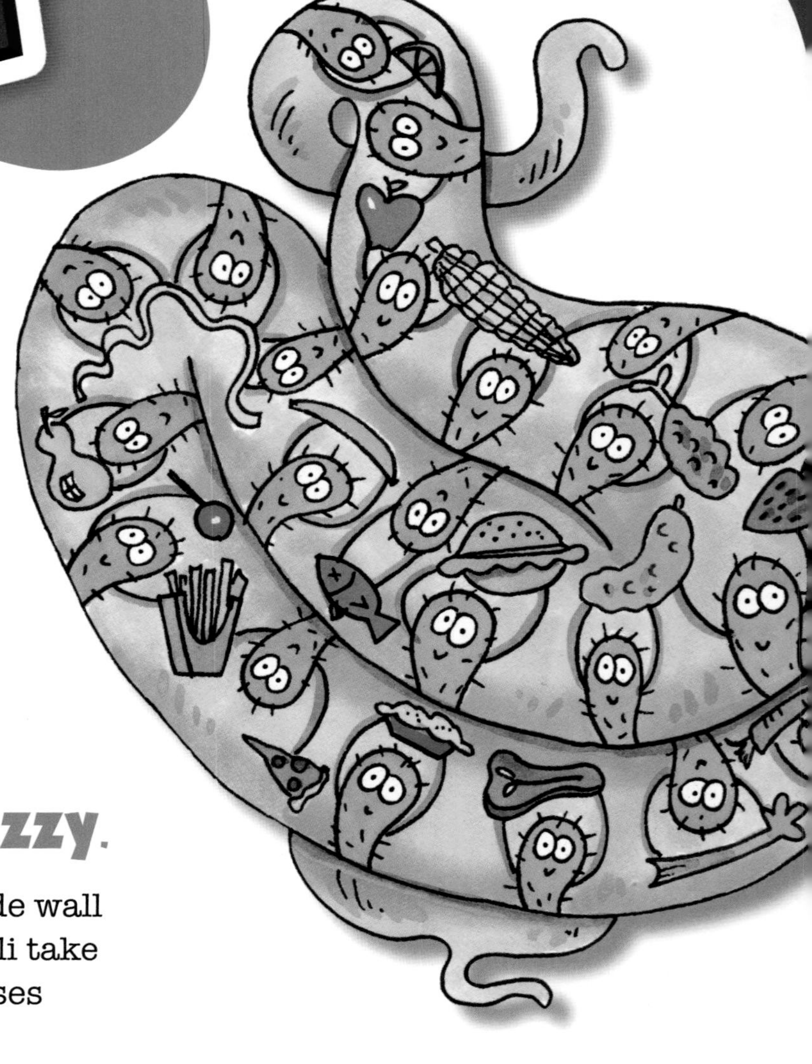

Your small intestines are fuzzy.

Tiny, hairlike **villi** line the inside wall of the small intestine. These villi take in nutrients from food as it passes through the digestive system.

Laid out, your blood vessels could wrap around the Earth more than two times.

There are 60,000 miles (97,000 km) of blood vessels in the average human body. Blood vessels carry blood and oxygen to and from your heart. They keep your body running!

An Iowa man named Charles Osborne had the hiccups for a world-record 68 years.

From 1922 to 1990, Osborne hiccupped an estimated 20 times per minute. His hiccups stopped for no known reason about a year before his death in 1991. Hiccups occur when a muscle **spasm** causes your **diaphragm** to contract suddenly.

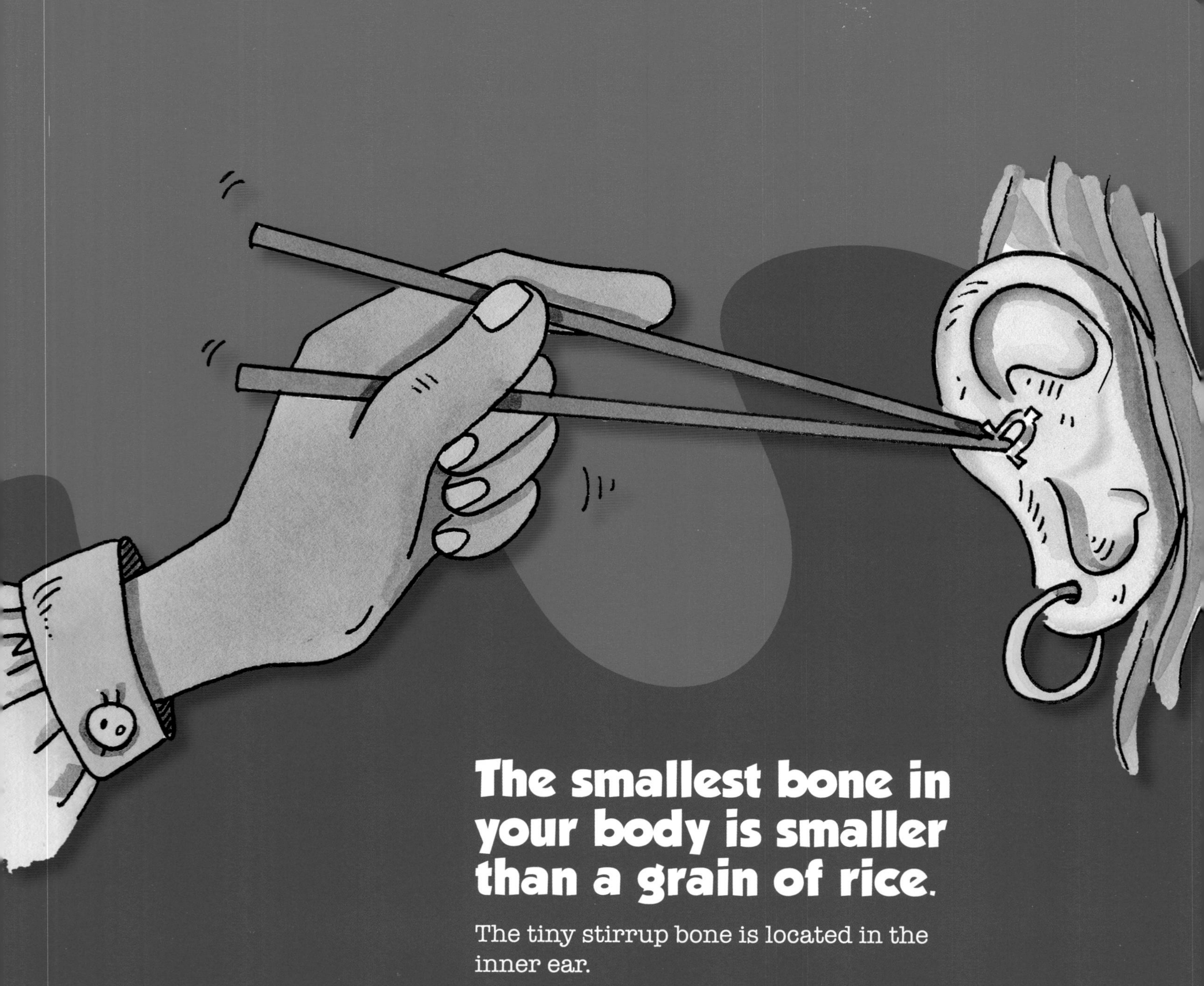

The smallest bone in your body is smaller than a grain of rice.

The tiny stirrup bone is located in the inner ear.

Human bones are stronger than concrete.

With lots of practice, some martial artists can break concrete, wood, bricks, and other hard objects with their bodies.

We lose bones as we grow.

Most babies are born with 350 separate bones. As we get bigger, some bones fuse together. By the time we're adults, we have only 206 bones.

Babies don't have kneecaps.

Humans are born with spongy cartilage where their kneecaps will be. By the time most kids are about two years old, this cartilage has hardened into bony kneecaps.

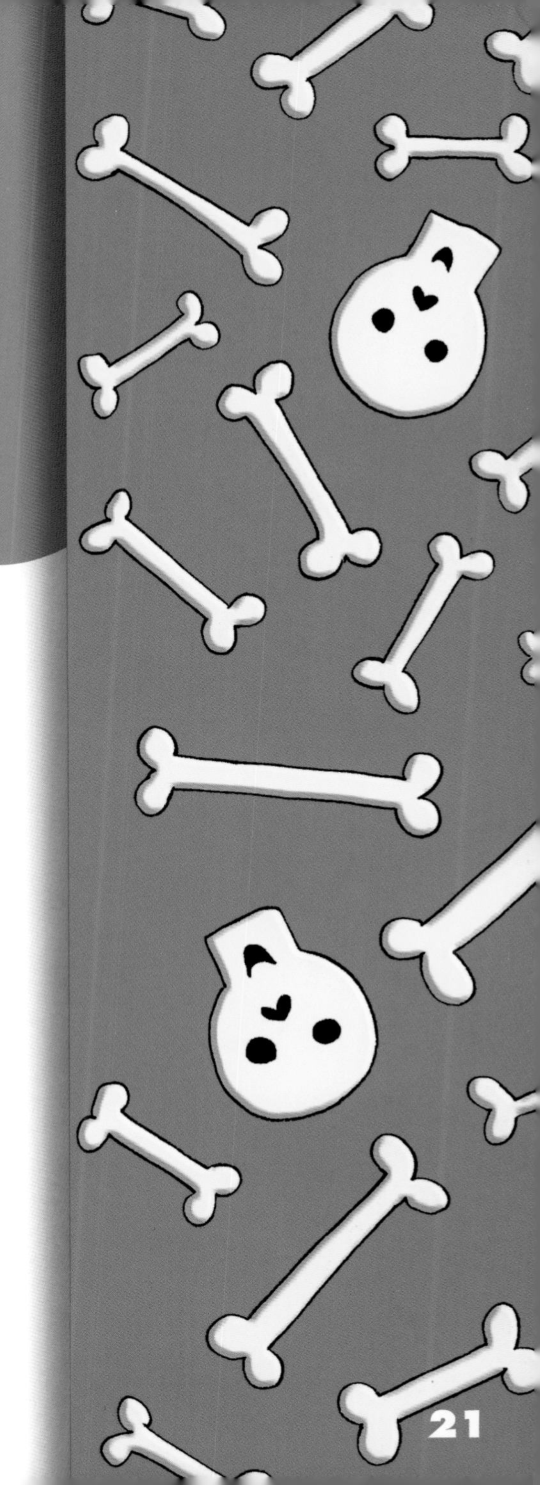

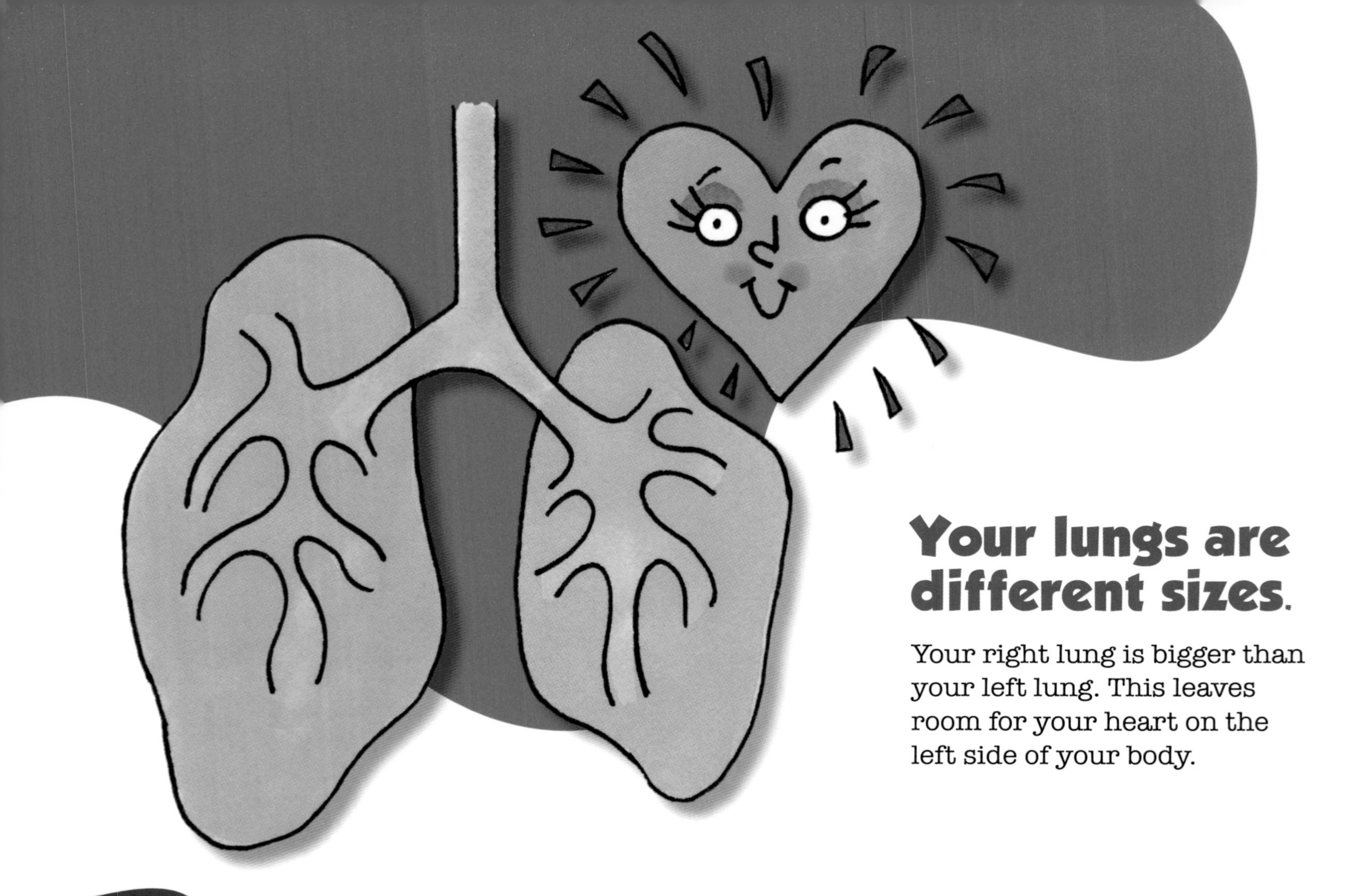

Your lungs are different sizes.

Your right lung is bigger than your left lung. This leaves room for your heart on the left side of your body.

Your heart uses electric signals to tell itself when to beat.

A heart beats when its walls contract, or pull in, then expand. This works like a pump and keeps your blood moving through your body.

You sit on the two largest muscles in your body.

The gluteus maximus helps you keep your balance, walk, run, and go up stairs.

The DNA in your body could reach the moon 6,000 times.

Stretched out, the DNA in a single human cell is 5 feet 7 inches (1.7 m) long.

You can scratch an itch in your sleep.

Itching often happens when nerves in your skin sense something new or unfamiliar. The nerves send signals to your brain, and your brain sends signals to your muscles to check out the unfamiliar feeling. This happens when you're awake and when you're asleep.

Skin is the largest organ of the human body.

Most adults have about 22 square feet (2 sq m) of skin weighing an average of 8 pounds (3.6 kg).

The average human sheds an entire layer of skin every two to four weeks.

This dead skin turns up as dust around your house, under your bed, and on your bookshelves.

Scratching makes mosquito bites itchier.

A mosquito's bite puts its saliva in its victim. This helps the mosquito drink your blood. The saliva causes a tiny infection in your body. Your body produces histamines, a type of chemical, to protect you. The histamines make you swell and itch. Scratching makes you produce more histamines, making the itching worse. Sooth the bite with ice or itch cream instead.

HANDS AND FEET

One fourth of the bones in your body are in your feet.

The best time to buy new shoes is in the afternoon.

Your feet swell and get slightly bigger throughout the day, so they are biggest in the afternoon. If you buy shoes first thing in the morning, you might end up with cramped feet later in the day.

Fingernails and toenails are made out of the same material as a bird's beak.

This substance is called **keratin**. This is the same material that makes up claws and horns in other animals.

The biggest feet in the world belonged to a man who was 8 feet 11.1 inches (2.7 m) tall.

Robert Wadlow of Illinois died in 1940, but his size 37 shoes are still on display in his hometown of Alton, Illinois. As of 2012, he was the tallest man in recorded history.

One in every 600 babies is born with more than ten fingers or toes.

This is due to a genetic condition called polydactyly. Most of the time the extra digits are very small or incomplete. But six-fingered humans have been musicians and baseball pitchers, including Antonio Alfonseca, who played Major League Baseball starting in the 1990s.

Your fingernails grow fastest in the summer.

They also grow more quickly on the hand you use the most. On average, fingernails grow about 1/10 inch (3/10 cm) each month. The nails on both your hands grow faster than toenails.

Identical twins have unique fingerprints.

Fingerprints are not genetic. Instead, they develop while a baby is still growing in its mother. Fluids, bone growth, and other factors shape fingerprints, so no two people have the same.

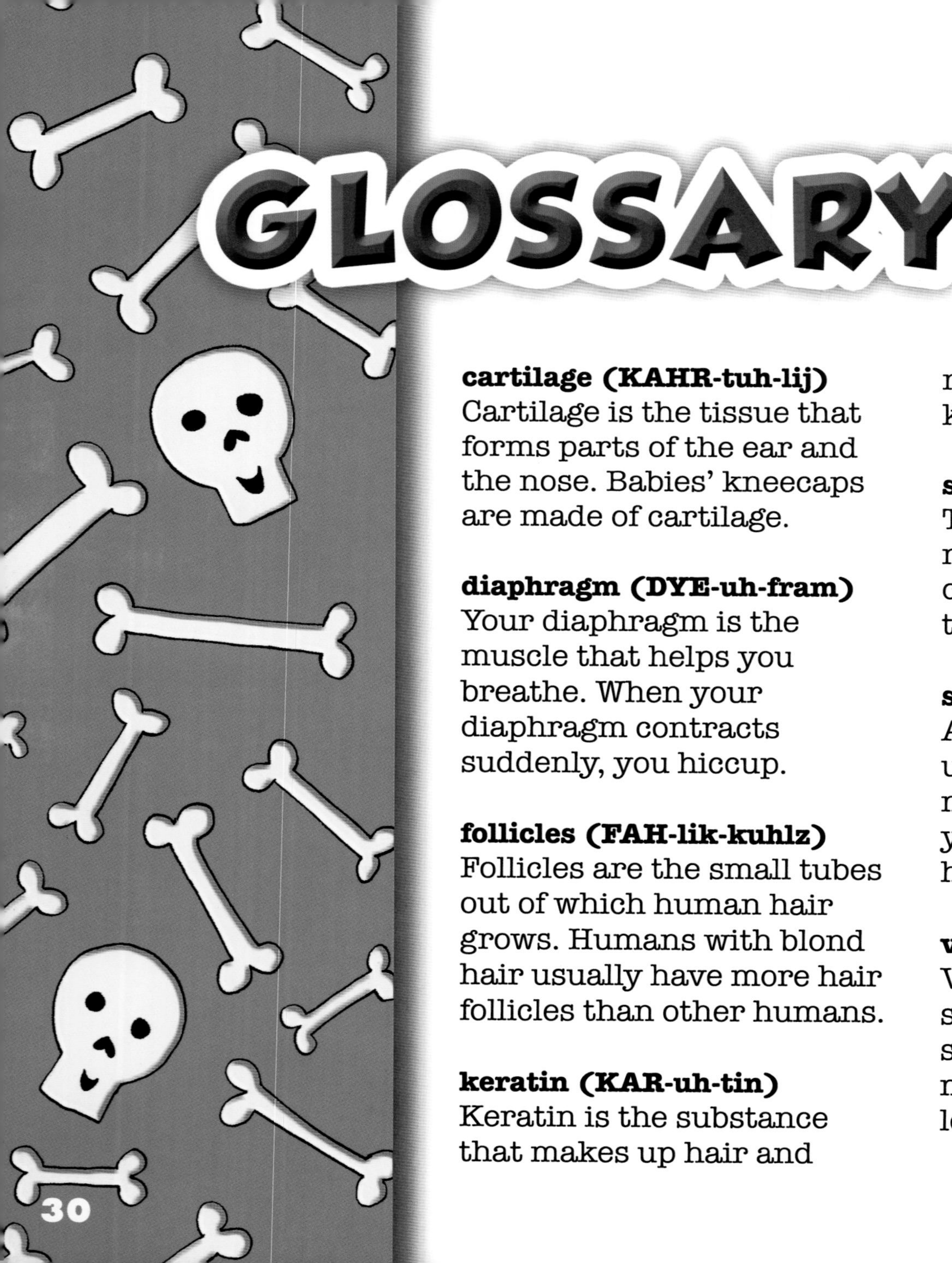

GLOSSARY

cartilage (KAHR-tuh-lij)
Cartilage is the tissue that forms parts of the ear and the nose. Babies' kneecaps are made of cartilage.

diaphragm (DYE-uh-fram)
Your diaphragm is the muscle that helps you breathe. When your diaphragm contracts suddenly, you hiccup.

follicles (FAH-lik-kuhlz)
Follicles are the small tubes out of which human hair grows. Humans with blond hair usually have more hair follicles than other humans.

keratin (KAR-uh-tin)
Keratin is the substance that makes up hair and nails. Bird beaks are made of keratin.

saliva (suh-LYE-vuh)
The water fluid in your mouth is saliva. One human can produce enough saliva to fill two swimming pools.

spasm (SPAZ-uhm)
A spasm is a quick, uncontrolled tightening of a muscle. A muscle spasm in your diaphragm can cause a hiccup.

villi (VIL-eye)
Villi are tiny fingerlike structures that line your small intestine. The villi make your small intestine look fuzzy.

LEARN MORE

BOOKS

Bingham, Jane. *The Human Body: from Head to Toe*. Chicago: Heinemann Library, 2004.

Beck, Paul, Tom Becker, and Mercer Mayer. *A Zombie's Guide to the Human Body: Anatomy 101 Taught By a Zombie.* New York: Scholastic, 2010.

Parker, Steve. *100 Facts on the Human Body*. Essex, UK: Bardfield Press, 2006.

WEB SITES

Visit our Web site for links about weird human body facts: **childsworld.com/links**

Note to Parents, Teachers, and Librarians: We routinely verify our Web links to make sure they are safe and active sites. So encourage your readers to check them out!

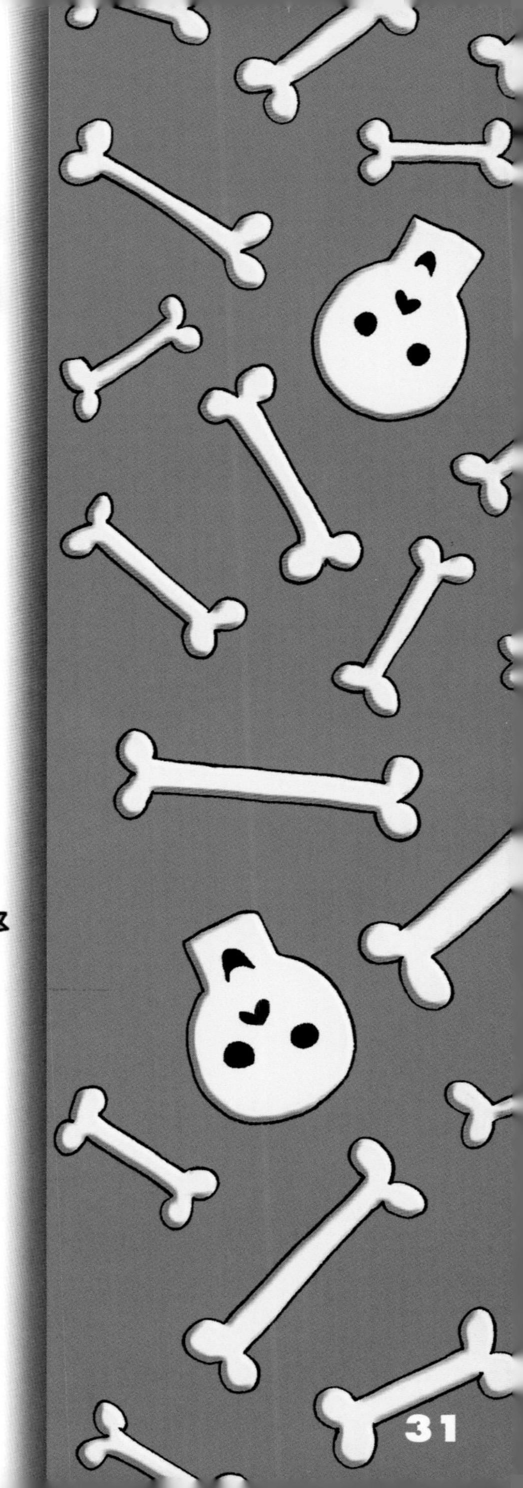

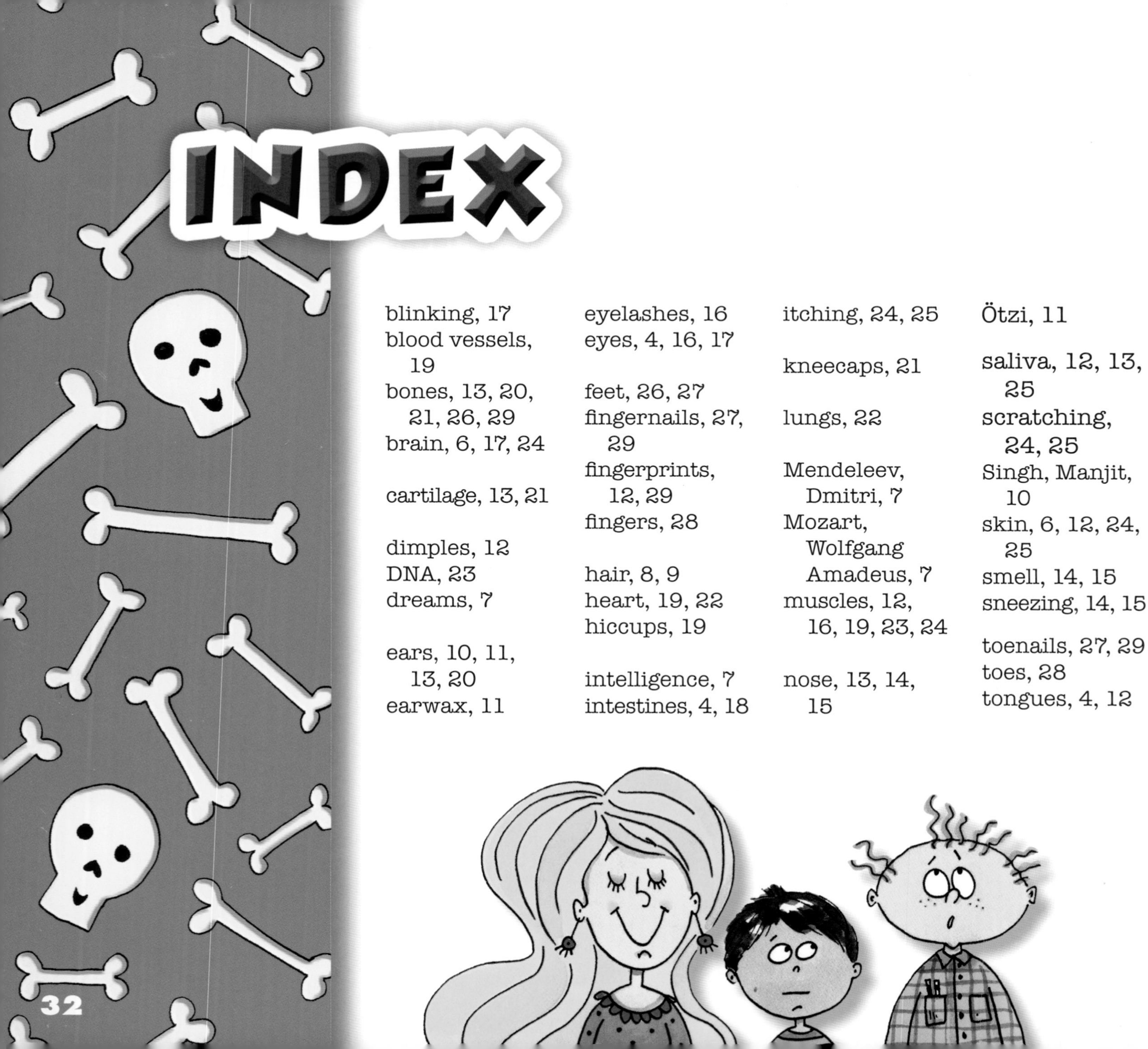

INDEX